eBay International Selling Made Easy

Contact me at

E-mail: hi@nickvulich.com
Blog: indieauthorstoolbox.com

Amazon Author Page:

- amazon.com/author/nickvulich
- amazon.com/author/nicholasvulich

Why you need to read this book

H ere's a secret many online sellers don't know. The fastest growing sellers on eBay are powering their growth with international sales. According to a recent article on *Linnworks*, "76% of [the] fastest growers are primarily trading across borders."

The beauty of selling internationally is when the domestic economy slows down and sales in your home country become sluggish, there are still pockets of growth and increasing demand in foreign economies. The key to tapping into these growth pockets is to make your items available to sellers in those countries.

I started listing items internationally in 2001. Within a year thirty to thirty-five percent of my sales came from international buyers. Over the last fourteen years I have completed nearly 5,000 international transactions.

If you're on the line about getting started with international selling—consider baby-stepping it. Start with proven foreign trade partners like Canada, the United Kingdom, and Australia. There are few language barriers dealing with these countries. You should also consider selling to Germany. According to a recent article in *Forbes Magazine*, Germany and the United Kingdom account for 48 percent of all international sales made on eBay.

Let's talk about that for a moment.

International sales are the fastest growing market segment on eBay and Amazon?

According to Google the population of the world is just over seven billion people. Roughly three hundred million of them live in the United States. That's slightly less than four percent of the world's population. Or, put another way—that means more than ninety-six percent of the world's population lives outside of the United States. And, they're all waiting to buy that exciting new widget you're getting ready to list.

I don't know about you, but that gets me excited! It makes me want to discover more about how I can tap into that market, and sell them more stuff.

. . . .

Before I go any further let me tell you a little more about me, so you can understand why I'm the right guy to help you grow your international sales on eBay.

Table of Contents

Why listen to me?

Hey there, Nick Vulich here.

If you're like me, I'm sure you're probably a little skeptical about taking advice from someone without knowing a little bit about them first.

I've been selling on eBay since 1999. Most of my online customers know me as history-bytes, although I've also operated as its old news, back door video, and sports card one.

I've sold 30,004 items for a total of $411,755.44 over the past fifteen years, and that's just on my history-bytes id. Right now I've cut way back on eBay selling to focus on my writing, but I still keep my hat in the game. That way I can stay current with the challenges my readers face every day when they go to sell on eBay.

I've been an eBay Power Seller or Top Rated Seller for most of the past fifteen years, which means I've met eBay's sales and customer satisfaction goals.

This is the eighth book I've written about selling on eBay. The first two, *Freaking Idiots Guide to Selling on eBay*, and *eBay Unleashed,* are aimed more towards how to get started selling on eBay. *eBay 2014* is directed at more advanced sellers and tackles many of the challenges top rated sellers face in the eBay marketplace. *eBay Subject Matter Expert* suggests a different approach to selling on eBay – building a platform where customers recognize you as an expert in your niche, and buy from you because of your knowledge in that field. *Sell It Online* gives a brief overview of selling on eBay, Amazon, Etsy, and Fiver. *How to Make Money Selling Old Books & Magazines on eBay* talks specifically about what I know best, how to sell books and magazines on eBay. *eBay Bookkeeping Made Easy* helps sellers understand how to keep track of the money they are making, and how to take advantage of the tax code to make even more money.

My most recent book, eBay 2015 is an attempt to tie it all together. Because people like short simple solutions to a single problem I've spun it off into three separate books —*eBay Bookkeeping Made Easy, eBay Shipping Simplified, and eBay International Selling Made Easy.*

It's info you need to know and apply today to thrive on eBay.

If you've already purchased *eBay 2015*, you have most of the information in this book. Save your $2.99, and grab a latte from Starbucks.

My goal is to help you become as successful as you wish to be.

Let's get started...

Sell International

To qualify for international visibility on eBay sellers must meet these requirements.

- Have a verified PayPal account tied to their eBay seller account

- PayPal must be offered as a payment option

- Must have 10 or more positive feedbacks

- Items must be listed in the appropriate category

- Need to enable shipping to countries you want to ship in

- For best visibility sellers must specify the levels of shipping service they are offering

If you sell using your eBay.com account, your feedback will be visible to sellers on eBay's foreign sites.

If you are a seller in the United States and specify you will ship to Canada, your items are automatically listed on eBay.ca.

Items listed on international sites do not count as duplicate listings, so sellers are not penalized for listing the same item on different eBay sites.

. . . .

eBay gives you four ways to make your items available to international buyers.

1. Opt into eBay's Global Shipping Program.
2. Enable your items for international shipping.
3. List your items on international sites.
4. Open eBay stores in countries where you do a large volume of business.

What I'm going to do next is look at each option in more detail and explain who it is for, and how you can get started using it.

eBay Global Shipping Program

S everal years ago eBay introduced their Global Shipping Program. It's an easy way for sellers to jump into international selling without having to worry about shipping rules, customs forms, etc.

If you've been itching to get started with international sales, but were afraid of the extra work involved I suggest giving it a shot using eBay's Global Shipping Program.

Many small sellers are terrified of international shipping. They've heard so many horror stories they're scared to give it a shot. They don't want to fill out customs forms, or worry about whether their package is going to make it all the way to Timbuktu or not.

eBay has eliminated all of that grief for sellers who use their Global Shipping Program. Sellers list their items just like they normally would. When the item sells they ship it to an eBay shipping center in the United States.

Bing badda boom! As soon as it arrives at the shipping center, your responsibility for the shipment is over. From that point on eBay and their shipping partners assume all responsibility for getting your package to its destination.

Here's how it works.

When you list your item for sale on eBay check the box to include your item in the Global Shipping Program and you're good to go.

Some categories don't qualify for inclusion in the Global Shipping Program. When you bump into these eBay will flag the item and let you know. I do a lot of selling in the collectibles category. Collectibles manufactured before 1899 don't qualify, so I see this issue pop up quite often. The only way around it is to ship the item internationally yourself. I'll discuss this option in more detail later.

When an item sells using the Global Shipping Program sellers can't send the buyer an invoice. eBay takes care of all this for you. The reason is you have no way of knowing what their shipping fee will be.

Once the customer pays you will receive a payment notice along with the address to ship your item to. An easy way to recognize a payment made through the Global Shipping Program is the address will include a long reference number.

Ship your item like you normally would. Include delivery confirmation so you can be sure the item was received at the shipping center. Once you have confirmation the item was received, your part in the transaction is complete.

eBay's shipping partner—Pitney Bowes—will readdress the item, fill out all of the appropriate customs forms, and ensure your item is delivered to the customer.

That's the way it should happen. Every now and then things don't work out as planned—the customer doesn't receive the item, or it arrives damaged. As a seller you're supposed to be protected from receiving negative feedback in such a situation. That's true to a point. You need to keep an eye on your feedback profile, and keep after eBay to update it when errors are made.

I received a negative feedback due to a customer not receiving their item. I knew it wasn't received, because that's what the seller wrote in his feedback. So I called eBay customer service and explained the problem. After about fifteen minutes of researching the problem the rep agreed I was not responsible. He removed the negative feedback while we were still on the phone.

If you experience a similar problem contact eBay customer service immediately. When you call have the listing item number and the feedback information available and ready to share with the rep you speak to. Make it easy for eBay to help you.

Overall the Global Shipping Program is a great way to increase your sales. At my peak selling period international sales accounted for roughly thirty-five to forty percent of my eBay sales and profits.

If you're looking for an effortless method to grow your sales opt into the Global Shipping Program and give it a shot.

Enable Items for International Shipping

We've already talked about eBay's Global Shipping Program and how easy it is to use, so why would anybody want to ship international packages on their own?

That's a great question.

It comes down to having more control over your shipping options, and the ability to make more sales. When you use the Global Shipping Program eBay adds in custom's fees, a markup to pay themselves and their shipping partner an additional profit, plus actual shipping costs. The final number eBay charges your customer for shipping can be mind-boggling, and can cost you the sale.

Let me use the products I sell as an example. When I ship items internationally on my own I charge $5.00 to ship items to Canada, and $9.00 for shipping anywhere else in the world. Sometimes I make a few extra bucks, sometimes I lose a few bucks, but over time it averages out. Keep in mind, the buyer is still responsible for duty and customs fees when their item arrives. Duties are taxes leveled by a customer's home country, and just like sales and income taxes—there's no getting around paying them.

When I sell using eBay's Global Shipping Program they charge my customer in the low twenty dollar range for shipping to Canada, and in the low thirty dollar range for shipping to Europe and the rest of the world. My items normally sell for sixteen to twenty-five dollars, so customers are confronted with some serious sticker shock when they're hit with eBay's shipping solution price.

Self-preservation is the primary reason I ship most international packages myself.

What I'm going to do now is walk you through setting up the international portion of your eBay sell your item form. It's structured very similar to how you set up your domestic shipping options so it should be easy to follow along and use.

. . . .

Everything you need to set your international shipping options can be found in the box labeled *International Shipping*.

The first choice you are offered is to opt into the Global Shipping Program. In this case you want to leave that box unchecked.

Below this you have a drop down menu that offers you the option to select flat rate, calculated shipping, or no additional options. As a quick review flat rate shipping is where you have one set shipping fee for all buyers, calculated shipping uses the eBay shipping calculator to determine the shipping price based upon where you are shipping your item to. The difference is— flat rate shipping is easier to set up and use, but calculated shipping can give buyers closer to you a break in shipping costs thus giving you the opportunity to grab additional sales from price conscious buyers.

After you choose your shipping method you'll see another drop down box that says shipping. It gives you three choices: worldwide, chose custom location, or Canada. I normally set up a separate price for worldwide and Canada— anymore is overkill in my book. However, if you ship a lot of packages to Mexico, the UK, or wherever go ahead and set up a special price for them too. The drop down box next to this lets you choose the type of service you wish to offer, and the box to the right of that lets you set your shipping price.

Below this you should see a line labeled *offer additional service*. You can use this to offer shipping to an additional location, or to offer a different delivery method.

In the *additional ship to locations* you can check off geographic areas you are willing to ship to. The buyer can then contact you for more details. Some sellers have lots of rules about where they will and will not ship too. A lot of sellers mark Malaysia, Italy, Mexico, Russia, etc. off limits because it's all over the internet other people have experienced problems when they ship packages there. In my book that's one of those urban legends—like the Chupacabra. I've shipped items to all of those countries and never had a problem. All I'm saying is if you're going to single out areas you won't ship to wait until you have a problem, then evaluate the situation and determine the best way to handle it.

The final line—combined shipping discounts, lets you apply your discount rules to this purchase if you set them up. My items are light and generally only add a few ounces to the package therefore I ship all additional items for free. It's a great way to encourage buyers to continue shopping with you. If you can't offer to ship all additional items for free—consider offering some type of discounted shipping for additional purchases. It will bring you more business over the long haul.

That's it. You're open for international business. Sit back and wait for the orders to role in.

I'm going to make one additional suggestion here. Take a few moments to help set buyer expectations. International buyers are similar to domestic buyers—they want to purchase their items today and receive them yesterday.

Ninety-nine times out of one hundred shipping goes smoothly and items arrive on time, but there are many circumstances beyond your control, especially when you're dealing with international customers.

I normally post the following information in each of my listings and include it again in my shipping emails.

"Normal international delivery time is eight to fifteen business days, but it can take as long as four to six weeks—depending upon customs and other shipping issues. Please be patient, and take this into consideration when placing your orders."

It helps to set buyer expectations before the order is placed. That way if the customer asks where their item is you can refer them back to the info posted in your listing. When you give realistic delivery time frames up front you save yourself a lot of grief and wasted emails trying to explain why customers haven't received their packages yet.

Remember—International customers really have you over the barrel. Tracking is virtually nonexistent for international shipments. The post office is experimenting with international delivery confirmation to select countries, but the service is spotty at best. There's no guarantee the mailman in Canada or the UK will actually scan your package when he drops it off. He may be having a bad day or he may be trying to outrun a dog. If your customer decides to file an item not received case you're going to lose because there's no way to provide proof of delivery.

Sorry to be the one to break it to you, but it's a fact of life when you're doing business on eBay. I've only had this happen once. A buyer in Germany opened an item not received case two days after paying for his item. There was no possible way it could travel from Iowa to Germany in two days.

Guess what? It didn't matter. eBay and PayPal decided the case against me because I didn't have proof of delivery. Like I said this happened one time out of five thousand international shipments so it's not a big deal. I spend more than that fueling my diet coke habit every week.

One other quick tip—many sellers assume proof of shipping is enough to win an international case. It's not. A stamped customs form from your post office doesn't mean anything if your buyer files an item not received case. If you can't show proof positive your item was delivered, you don't have a leg to stand on.

List Your Items on International Sites

What we've talked about so far involves listing your items on eBay.com, and making them available to buyers in foreign countries. The reason this works is eBay.com is the largest of the eBay sites and has the most listings posted to it. As a result many international buyers search here first when they're looking for new items.

If you do a lot of business with certain countries you may be able to increase sales there by listing items directly on that site.

If you're a registered eBay user you can sell on any of eBay's international sites. To get started just log in with your current ID and password, and start listing your items. Sellers with anchor stores can list on international sites for free. Sellers without an anchor store are charged listing fees if they exceed their free limits

If you want to make more sales there are a few details you should consider.

(1.) What language are you going to post your listings in?

If you're selling in Canada, the United Kingdom, or Australia—English might be fine. But, the UK and Australia use different dialects, and the meanings for words are not always the same. Canada has a large French speaking population so you need to consider them, too. Should you post in English and French?

If you're posting your listing in Germany, France, or Japan—what do you do? Many of the buyers there speak English as a second language, but do you want to leave their understanding to chance?

It's a tough call. You can use Google Translate or Bing Translate to write your description. The translations are usually stilted, and hard to read. A better choice would be to find a native language translator on Fiverr or odesk. They would be able to provide you with a more accurate translation.

If you're selling low dollar value or one-of-a-kind items the translation apps are going to be your most cost effective option. If you're setting up more expensive items you are going to sell over and over again, a good translator can help you create more professional sounding listings that will make more sales. Look at it as an investment in your success.

Other sellers choose to rely on translation apps that let potential buyers select the language they want to read the description in. eBay offers several of these apps that you can place in your item description. One app is called *One Hour Translation* and the other is *Translation for Worldwide*. You can read more about them in the app guide at the end of this chapter.

2. What about your title? Are the keywords and the context the same in German, Spanish, and other languages as they are in the United States?

Do you know what terms someone in Germany would use to search for an iPad, or a smart phone? When they're looking for a denim jacket, what other terms would they search by?

Your title is how potential buyers discover your item. If you don't know the local dialect or slang, how do you know the best words to use in your title?

Go back to item one. A translator fluent in the native language would be able to write the most appropriate title for your item listings.

3. What are you going to charge for shipping?

Do you charge international rates, offer free shipping, or split it somewhere in the middle?

Shipping is a key ingredient in determining how successful you'll be at international selling. The good news is items just about always make it to their destination. The bad news is sometimes packages take forever to arrive at their destination.

When I listed items on the eBay.uk site several years ago I marked my items up a bit and offered free shipping. A funny thing happened—most of my items ended up selling to my regular customers here in the United States. It wasn't quite what I expected, but sales did go up.

After a month or two, I switched tactics and offered a low cost international shipping option—five dollars, compared to the nine dollar rate I charged on eBay.com. Once I did that I started getting more buyers from the U. K.

Joseph Dattilo, founder of Virtualbotix, LLC, says –

"We offer USPS and UPS shipping providers and generally have First Class International, Priority International, Priority Express International, and UPS International as an option. Initially we only had First Class International as an option, but found that very few high value items sold, and we were contacted by dozens of buyers who demanded that we make other methods available.

"Since offering USPS Priority Mail International and USPS Priority Mail express International we have seen a dramatic increase in sales of items whose value is greater than $100. The interesting thing is that the boost to sales occurred, but the use of these more expensive services is still rather rare. Customers seem more likely to buy knowing they have the option to get it fast, but often still choose the most economical shipping method…"

The final takeaway is sellers can benefit from offering a larger variety of shipping options, even if their customers decide not to take advantage of them.

4. How are you going to approach delivery time?

Even if you explain that your item ships from the United States, many buyers aren't going to understand. What they're going to see is your item is listed on their home site—eBay.uk or eBay.de.

Shipping time is a tough call with any international shipping method. A lot of my First Class shipments make it to Europe faster than similar items take to ship across the state. Others seem like they get buried on the proverbial slow boat to China.

The problem is, as a seller, you have no way of knowing which packages are going to get tied up in customs. The best you can do is help to set reliable delivery expectations for your customers.

Offer your customers a variety of mailing options—First Class International, Priority International, and Priority Express International, then give them time frames for delivery using each service. Tell customers the longest it should take for items to deliver. Most often their package will arrive sooner, and customers will be delighted because the item was delivered sooner than they expected.

5.) Are you going to price your item in U S dollars, Pounds Sterling, or Euros?

If you're selling on eBay.uk or eBay.de and you price your item in dollars it's going to confuse buyers. If you price your item in Pounds Sterling or Euros you're going to have to keep a close eye on currency fluctuations to make sure you don't end up taking a bath if the market turns. When you go to pull your money out of PayPal, it's a two-step process. You have to convert your currency to U S dollars first, and then you can transfer funds to your bank.

6.) What are you going to tell your customers about VAT taxes, customs fees, and duty fees?

Many customers aren't going to understand why they have to pay extra fees and taxes. When you list items on their home site they don't associate the purchase triggering additional fees for customs and duty.

To prevent negative feedback and multiple returns you need to explain in every listing that your item ships from the United States and customers are responsible for all customs and duty fees as well as VAT taxes. You need to include the same information in every shipping email.

Joseph Dattilo, of Virtuabotix, says they adhere to eBay's policy on every international listing and include the following disclaimer in every item description –

"For international orders (outside of the United States of America) please allow for additional time for your products to arrive, or choose one of our expedited services to ensure your product arrives in a timely manner. Basic international shipping can take as much as 30 to 60 days depending on your country while expedited international shipments have guaranteed delivery windows.

"Import duties, taxes, and charges are not included in the item price or shipping cost. These charges are the buyer's responsibility.

"Please check with your country's customs office to determine what these additional costs will be prior to bidding or buying."

All sellers should include similar wording in their international listings. If you don't include similar wording, eBay may decide a case against you if a customer opens a buyer protection case against you citing extended delivery times or additional fees for customs.

Open an International eBay Store

If you're serious about international selling, and have a target market in mind, it might make sense to open an international eBay store.

Let's say you're doing a booming business selling vintage concert t-shirts. Your two best international markets are Germany and the United Kingdom. You've just picked up a new line of custom printed t-shirts, hoodies, bikinis, and other apparel items. The new items are selling well to buyers who like the vintage look, but can't lay down several hundred dollars for a vintage t-shirt.

You know from experience the majority of customers who buy your vintage look apparel discover it in your eBay store. Sales in the U. K. and Germany aren't taking off, but your marketing intern had a light bulb moment—What if you opened local eBay stores in those markets so you could cross promote the vintage look apparel?

Bingo!

The best way to grow an international market is the same way you do it at home. Build an eBay store, and cross promote your items.

Set up a scrolling gallery at the bottom of every listing that features the vintage look apparel. Mention the vintage look apparel in every listing, and invite customers to explore your eBay store for more great deals.

Set up listing headers that feature the new items. Build a store front with clickable links to the new categories. Make it bold. Make it visual.

Use markdown Manager to your advantage. Offer free shipping occasionally. Discount a different category every week or every month. Set up promotion boxes to highlight your specials.

If you're setting up an eBay store in a non-English speaking country, find a translator to set up your listings and titles.

. . . .

An eBay store is a slightly more expensive way to sell international, but the payoff could be immense if you can make a go of it.

The key to success is to localize the store to each market you sell in, cross promote items as much as possible, and run frequent specials to build your brand.

eBay Apps to Grow Your Business

Currency Converter

By 3D Sellers

. Let's buyers calculate auction prices in the currency of their choice.

Blog Post

By PMIT Inc.

. This app turns your eBay listings into blog posts so you can share them across your social media sites.

Endicia Int'l. Advisor

By Endicia.com

. Gives you the info you need to manage your international shipments. Helps you understand international shipping requirements to various countries, rates for different shipping classes, and expected delivery times.

Ship Saver Insurance

By Inkfrog

. Discount insurance for international shipments. At the time of this writing (2014), you can insure USPS First Class shipments for $1.10 per $100 of value up to $1000.

My Store Maps

By My Store Credit, Inc.

. Place world maps in your item descriptions to show buyers locations you have previously shipped to. Some sellers say the visual representation encourages customers to order from them.

Webgistix GlobalFill

By Webgistix Corporation

. Allows sellers outside of the United States to print bar coded mailing labels for shipments into the United States. The claim is that the bar codes can reduce shipping time by up to five days.

One Hour Translation

By 3D Seller

. A translation widget you can add to your listings that supports up to twelve languages.

Translator for Worldwide

By PMIT Inc.

. A translation app you can include in your eBay listings. Currently supports 60 languages.

. . . .

Apps can help you make more sales. They can help you manage different aspects of your eBay business such as bookkeeping, social media updates, blogging, translations, etc.

Apps can also turn your listings into a waste dump.

One problem I've encountered using apps on eBay is it's impossible to completely eliminate them if you choose to stop using the app. I used One Hour Translation at the top of my listing for a while. Several months later when I stopped using it, the visible part of the app was taken out of my listings, but it was replaced with a blank space where the translation app used to appear.

I had the same problem when I used a social media app. When I stopped using it, the app was replaced with a blank space at the top of all my listings.

The only way to completely remove the app is to go into each item description page and manually strip out the HTML code.

Best advice: Think hard before adding any apps to your eBay listings.

Interview with Joseph Dattilo on International Shipping

(This is an extract of an interview with Joseph Dattilo of Virtuabotix. They sell on eBay, Amazon, and from their own website https://www.virtuabotix.com/. Joseph is the founder of Virtuabotix, LLC, and handles much of the international selling for his company. His take on international selling should help both new and existing eBay sellers.)

Joseph Dattilo of Virtuabotix

Could you tell me a little bit about why you don't use the Global Shipping Program?

By the time the Global Shipping Program was a consideration we already had started shipping internationally from both Amazon and our own Website. Because of the fees and other restrictions we opted to streamline shipping with our own process.

One problem I've encountered with the program is sticker shock for my customers. When eBay includes their fees, shipping charges, customs, etc. the price is often three or four times what I normally charge. Is that similar to your findings?

In our experience the lower cost we can provide as an option for shipping, the more likely we will make the sale. Increasing the cost to international buyers did not seem like a viable strategy since we are able to maintain less than $10 shipping rates for basic international orders by shipping and insuring directly. Our estimates placed the cost at well around the 2 to 3 times mark if we used the Global Ship Program.

One concern everyone has is tracking with international shipments. What shipping services do you use? What has

been your experience with tracking, or do you even worry about it?

We offer UPS and USPS shipping providers, and generally have First Class International, Priority International, Priority Express International, and UPS International as an option. Initially we only had First Class International as an option. But we found very few high value items sold. We were contacted by dozens and dozens of buyers who demanded we make other shipping methods available.

Since offering both USPS Priority Mail International, and USPS Priority Mail Express International we have seen a dramatic increase in sales of items whose value is greater than $100. The interesting thing is the boost to sales occurred, but the use of these more expensive services are still rather rare. Customers appear more likely to buy knowing they have the option to get it fast, but most still choose the most economical shipping method.

Even if you pay for tracking, a lot of times you can't actually track your packages. Priority Mail Express International is completely un-trackable outside of the US (despite what is advertised by the postal service).

You mention international shipping is about 25% of your business? Are those numbers fairly consistent for you, or are they seasonal?

For our business there has always been a fairly large amount of international interest, so the ratio is fairly consistent regardless of time of year. The only time when that is not the case is during the holidays (October to January). US sales greatly increase on all channels during that time period.

Which countries are your buyers coming from now?

Canada, Australia, and most of the Euro zone countries perform fairly well. There's also a strong market in Brazil, Chile, and several other South American countries.

It is likely that our sales in Spanish speaking countries would improve if we made a Spanish version of our listings available.

Do you use eBay's international visibility program, or do you just enable international shipping?

We simply enable international shipping at this point, and we seem to be selling well in international markets.

You said you also sell on Amazon and from your own website. How do international sales from those sites compare to eBay?

International performance is very strong on eBay and Virtuabotix.com, especially when compared to Amazon. One reason for this is Amazon forces you to provide only two methods of international shipping. That means the only two options we can provide are standard, and the most expensive shipping option. This also makes it difficult to list things with LIPO batteries that have to have customized shipping rules and require UPS shipping (which is extremely expensive).

I know a lot of sellers who shy away from international shipping because of all of the horror stories they've heard about packages getting lost, stolen, etc. Do you have a big problem with international shipments going astray? or are your numbers similar to those for domestic packages?

International orders and customers can be as difficult as the stories make them out to be—sometimes. And, there are some problem orders, but when you consider only 1 in 200 orders tends to have problems (caused by the post office) it's still a fairly good track record.

We used to have a lot more problems with international customers, but that was primarily due to poor communications, and customers not having clear delivery expectations. Some of the worst situations with international order disputes were because it was not clear how long standard orders can take to deliver. Delivery can take as long as 30 to 60 days (It's always better to overestimate).

An even worse problem is first time international buyers who are outraged by having to pay VAT taxes and other import fees specific to their country.

In order to address a lot of those problems we put the verbiage below to help. The part about import duties and taxes is required to be inside your listing verbatim to fit the guidelines eBay requires to remove negative feedback that specifically relates to VAT & other Taxes or duties.

International Buyers – Please Note:

For international order (outside of the United States of America) please allow for additional time for your products to arrive, or choose one of our expedited services to ensure your product arrives in a timely manner. Basic International shipping can take as much as 30 to 60 days depending on your country while expedited international shipments have guaranteed delivery windows.

Import duties, taxes, and charges are not included in the item price or shipping cost. These charges are the buyer's responsibility.

You mention Spanish speaking countries would probably bring you more sales if you spent extra time on them. Have you tried listing directly on those sites, or opening an international store in the countries you sell in.

We have identified some of our top markets, and would like to translate out listings and site into Spanish to help those customers use our products, and give greater levels of exposure in those countries. At such a time that we have those translations available we would likely create specific listings for those sites. We are also looking for distributors in those countries who can ship locally since that is often more desirable for individuals in those countries, and would reduce the impact of international shipping costs and delays on conversions for our products.

When you sell on international sites, is currency fluctuation a problem, or do you list your items in U S Dollars?

In general we list our items in US Dollars. Currency fluctuation has a greater impact on our cost of goods sold than it does on our per sale revenue. Ensuring our shipping prices are both reasonable, and adequate enough to cover all costs have a much more significant effect since shipping prices increase dramatically as weight and volume increases. It is easy to lose money if you do not set your shipping prices appropriately.

Despite what is advertised by the postal service international tracking doesn't always happen. Is that a problem for you as far as refunds and other customer service issues? Or do you just give a refund when a customer complains, and move on to the next sale?

Our responsibility to our customer does not end until our products have reached and satisfied the technical needs of our customers. Generally when a problem arises with international shipping where a product has not arrived and it is outside or near the maximum time range expected for the service selected, we simply send a replacement or refund the purchase as appropriate. It is very important to collect messages from your buyers with the statement that they never received your product, and to file a claim report as soon as possible providing this evidence to your insurance company in order for insurance payments to be approved. Failure to provide written proof of non-delivery or damage can cost you a lot.

Generally the idea is to make sure your customer knows you trust that they are having a genuine problem and that you are eager and willing to fix it. Ask for a confirmation of delivery address, and a clear statement of the un-delivered or damaged goods (a picture in the case of damage is often required). Finally you provide the replacement or refund as agreed upon between you and the customer. In the background, you will then submit a claim and wait the long period (often over 90 days) for your claim to be approved and paid. Trying to make one of your customers wait for the insurance to kick in is a recipe for disaster, after-all it's not their fault (even if it is :D).

eBay has had a number of self-inflicted problems over the last four months. Of course, they had the security breach for both eBay and PayPal, and have forced users to change their passwords. eBay also eliminated all of their Google AdWords this year, and soon afterwards they were busted by Google for practicing Black Hat SEO tactics. As a result Google removed a lot of eBay listings from search. How has this affected your business? Has it slowed sales, or caused other problems?

Because of our multi-channel approach an adverse effect on eBay has a positive effect on Amazon or Virtuabotix.com. An adverse effect on Amazon has a positive effect on eBay or Virtuabotix.com, and you guessed it...an adverse effect on Virtuabotix.com usually results in a positive effect on eBay or Amazon.

Overall we have had a much more pleasant experience with eBay then Amazon, and we genuinely feel like eBay cares about having our products on their site. In contrast selling electronics on Amazon can be a nightmare, and we have had to spend a great deal of time and money dealing with Amazon policies that are designed more to benefit Amazon than anyone else. The ability to brand your business on eBay as compared to the outright banning of the practice on Amazon also plays a large factor in the value that eBay can provide to a business.

Overall despite any recent problems that eBay may have encountered, we at Virtuabotix.com still feel that our relationship with eBay has tons of potential for growth, and that the overall most Americans in need of our Electronics, and Robotics equipment have a positive view of the purchasing experience that shopping Virtuabotix through eBay provides them.

Customs Forms

The easiest way to handle customs forms is by using online shipping tools. When you use the online tools available through eBay, Click-N-Ship, Endicia, or Stamps.com they automatically walk you through the forms and ensure they are filled out correctly.

For those of you who insist on doing it old style here's a quick tutorial on customs forms.

The post office uses two customs forms—form 2976 and form 2976-A. Form 2976 is required on all international packages weighing less than four pounds. Form 2976-A is required for all international packages weighing more than four pounds.

Form 2976

Form 2976

The key information needed for each form is –

- Sender's address
- Recipient address
- Value of each item enclosed
- Total value of all items enclosed
- Description of contents
- Senders signature

You are given several choices to describe the contents including: gift, document, commercial sample, other. You need to check other, and then describe the contents in the description box.

Oftentimes sellers will ask you to lie about the value or check the gift box so they don't have to pay duty fees (taxes). Be aware that if you are caught doing this it is a felony—subject to fines and jail time. If you're tempted to fudge the form for them, ask yourself—is the extra sale worth the penalties you could face?

That's pretty much all there is to it.

Have the post office walk you through your first customs form. After doing it once or twice you'll be a pro and wonder why you ever worried about international shipping.

Form 2976 A

Form 2976A

Remember form 2976 A is for international packages that weigh over four pounds, or contain contents valued at over $400.

The key information needed to fill out form 2976 A is –

- Sender's address
- Recipient address
- Value of each item enclosed
- Total value of all items enclosed
- Description of contents
- Senders signature

You are given several choices to describe the contents including: gift, document, commercial sample, other. You need to check other, and then describe the contents in the description box.

Printing International Postage with Stamps.com

eBay's shipping label service is great, but sometimes you need a little more oomph to boost your sales and simplify things even more.

I've been using Stamps.com for nearly ten years and it's been a great alternative for me. Other people have had good luck using Endicia to handle their shipping needs. Both services charge a monthly service fee for using them.

I know what you're thinking. Wait a minute Nick, I'm trying to save money, not spend even more.

Believe me, I understand. The thing is I actually save a lot of money using Stamps.com to power my eBay shipping. Here's why I use it, and how it saves me money.

What got me hooked on Stamps.com is it's the only way I can ship my items first class international without going to the post office and having them print labels for me. If you use eBay's shipping solution or Click-N-Ship® you can only ship internationally using priority or express mail. When I do that, international sales go down because of the extra shipping costs involved. The extra sales I get by offering the less expensive shipping solution more than cover the $15.99 monthly fee.

One of the other reason I like using Stamps.com is it collects information from all of the platforms I sell on and lets me handle all of my shipping from one central location. For me, that means I can ship the items I sell on eBay, Amazon, bid Start, and my own website all from the same program console.

I don't have to jump from site to site to ship everything. If I need to look up shipping info for an item—it's all in Stamps.com.

It's convenient. I like that. It's worth the extra fifteen dollars a month it costs me to use the service.

International Shipping with Stamps.com

Setting up an order for international delivery is very similar to shipping a domestic order. The only difference is you need to complete a customs form.

Here what you need to do to fill out the online customs form.

Click on the customs form, and it will display a pop up box for you to fill out. At the top of the form it asks for a phone number. If your customer listed a number with eBay it will prepopulate. If they did not give a phone number I just fill in 999-999-9999, otherwise it will not let you continue.

Where it asks for contents you are given several options. Choose <merchandise>. In the box next to this type a short description. I usually type article or print.

About midway down the page there is a section labeled *itemized package contents*. The first box asks for the quantity or number of items in your package. After that you're asked for a short description of the item. It should prepopulate from your eBay item description. If the description is too long you need to shorten it, or the form will not process properly. The next item it asks you for is the weight of just the item (without the packaging).

When you've completed all of the items the box at the end of this line asks *add item*. Check that box, and it will move your description into the box below that line.

At the bottom of the pop up box is a form you need to check. It begins with "I acknowledge…" Once you select the check box, the pop up box disappears, and you can print your item like normal.

Final takeaway: Stamps.com is easy to use, and takes all of the hassle out of international shipping. It fills out, and prints the customs labels for you. You can't ask for anything more than that from a computer application.

Bonus - Excerpt From eBay Ninja Tips & Tricks

(Here's a short excerpt from my book eBay Ninja Tips and Tricks, Save Time, Increase Sales, Make More Money. It's packed with tips to help you supercharge your eBay sales.)

1) **Attach a domain name to your eBay store**. A domain gives your eBay store a professional touch. You can add your domain name to your email signature, Facebook page, and Twitter profile—wherever you're seen online and offline.

It's easy to do, and normally costs under twenty dollars per year.

The easiest way to get started is by using **WWW Domain for My Store**. It's available as an app in the eBay Applications tab on your My eBay page. The current cost is $17.95 per year.

Sure, you can purchase your domain name cheaper using Go Daddy, e nom, or other registrars, but when you do that, you need to set up your domain forwarding services yourself. It's not hard, but it's an extra step that prevents a lot of sellers from adding a domain name to their eBay store. When you register with WWW Domain for My Store the app does all of this for you.

2) **Write Reviews & Guides**. Take a few minutes out to write reviews and guides about a few of the items you sell. They will help customers to see you as an expert in what you sell, and they have links back to your eBay store. More eyes on your eBay store should mean more sales. Share your knowledge, grow your business.

3) **Keep an eye on your competition**. If you really want to grow your business on eBay, you need to know who your competition is. Set aside fifteen or twenty minutes every week to see what your competition is doing. Look at what they're selling, the type of pictures they are using, how much they're charging for shipping. Take a look at their prices. Are you're prices competitive? Maybe you can raise your prices a few bucks, or maybe you need to lower prices a little to stay competitive. You also want to pay close attention to what your competitors are selling. Have they recently added new products? Have they dropped a product line altogether? Maybe you should do the same thing? Watch for trends in what your competition is doing. It will help you grow your business.

4) **Put You Tube videos in your listings**. It's a fact, people are hooked on video. Look for ways to include video in your listings. Include a short video about your business. If you sell items that need installation or set up, link to You Tube videos that show how to do it. Make a short series of how to videos about how to use your products, and post links to them in you eBay listings.

5) **Shop Uline for packing supplies**. If you ship in bulk Uline offers some of the best prices you're going to find on packaging supplies. They sell boxes, stay-flat mailers, Tyvek envelopes, peanuts, tape, labels just about anything you need. Depending upon where you're located, you can order today, and have your shipping supplies tomorrow. Having said that, don't forget to check for the same items on eBay. Sometimes eBay sellers offer better prices than Uline.

6) **Order free packing supplies from the Post Office**. Don't buy your boxes, get them for free. That's right. The post office will provide you with free boxes and mailers when you ship with priority and express mail. Better yet, you can order them online, and they will deliver them to your home for free.

7) **Source product to resell on eBay**. Before you go running all over searching for product to resell, take a few moments to check out what's for sale on eBay. I've sold over $400,000 on

eBay in the past fourteen years. I purchased over 95% of it on eBay; repackaged it, and sold it for twenty times what I originally paid.

8) **Only closed auctions count**. People ask all sorts of crazy prices for things on eBay. Just remember, asking and getting are two different things. When you research products and pricing on eBay, remember only closed items count. They tell you what people actually paid for something; what the starting price was; and what type of pictures, descriptions, and titles are effective.

9) **Use separate accounts to buy and sell**. Things happen. Sales go wrong. Tempers flare up. One of the outcomes can be bad feedback. Why risk receiving bad feedback on your seller account? Set up a separate account for personal purchases. It will make tracking business expenses easier, and it will prevent problems that may bring you bad feedback.

10) **Drop shipping is a scam**. There are a lot of books out there that tell you how drop shipping is the greatest thing ever. You can sell TV's, phones, and all sort of products with no risks. Just list the item, purchase it when you make a sale. Don't get taken in by the hype. A lot of eBay sellers have ruined their reputations using drop shippers. Products ship late; products are out of stock; or they ship the wrong item. Next thing you know you've got a load of bad feedback. The first tip off drop shipping

is a bad deal; they charge you $100 to $500 to join their circle of sellers.

11) **Be careful selling from wholesaler catalogs**. I had the brilliant idea one time to resell products from the LTD catalog. Fortunately I checked the items I wanted to sell on eBay first. Most of the items were being sold at or below the catalog price, as sellers tried to recover a portion of what they spent. Lesson learned: Research everything. Don't buy product and expect to make a profit; buy product when you're sure you're going to make a profit.

12) **Set up your profile page**. People like to know who they're doing business with. Make it easy for them to trust you. Post a picture of yourself. Share a little information about yourself, and what got you started selling on eBay. If you're a specialist in your product line, tell people about it. Not everyone is going to look at your profile page, but for those who do it will reassure them you are a good guy.

13) **Shop clearance sales**. Next time you go shopping at Walmart, Target, TJ Maxx, or any retail store, take a stroll through the clearance aisles. There are a lot of eBay sellers who make their entire living from the items they find in the clearance aisles. Add the eBay app to your cell phone, and check a few items to see what they're selling for on eBay.

Before You Go

Thank you for reading this book. If you enjoyed it, or found it helpful, I'd be grateful if you'd post a short review where you purchased it. Your review really does help. It helps other readers decide if this book would be a good investment for them, and it helps me to make this an even better book for you. I personally read all of the reviews my books receive, and based on what readers tell me, I can make my books even better, and include the kind of information readers want and need.

Thanks again for choosing my book, and here's wishing you great sales on eBay.

Nick Vulich

Kindle Unlimited

kindleunlimited

Freedom to Explore

Remember—**if you're a Kindle Unlimited subscriber you can read this book and many of my other books for free**.

To read this book for free, select **read for free** in the order box and it will be delivered to your Kindle reading device for absolutely no charge.

Here are some of my other eBooks available through Kindle Unlimited.

Writing As Nick Vulich

- eBay 2015
- eBay 2014
- Sell It Online
- eBay Shipping Simplified
- eBay Bookkeeping Made Easy
- Etsy Bookkeeping Made Easy
- How to Make Money Selling Old Books & Magazines on eBay
- eBay Unleashed

- Freaking Idiots Guide to Selling on eBay
- Freaking Idiots Guide to Fiver
- eBay Ninja Tips & Tricks
- eBay Subject Matter Expert
- Make $1000 Selling on eBay Before Christmas
- Kindle Cash System
- Indie Author's Toolbox
- Life Without the BS
- 7 Steps to A New Job
- Fit After Fifty

Writing As Nicholas L. Vulich
- Killing the Presidents
- Killing President Lincoln
- Bad Ass Presidents
- Andrew Jackson: Old Hickory
- Abraham Lincoln: The Baltimore Plot
- Manage Like Abraham Lincoln

Writing As Braun Schweiger
- $100,000 eBay Business
- eBay 30 Day Challenge
- eBay Selling Made Easy

Books by Nick Vulich

eBay 2014: Why You're Not Selling Anything on eBay, and What you Can Do About it

Freaking Idiots Guide to Selling on eBay: How Anyone Can Make $100 or More Everyday Selling on eBay

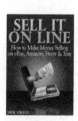

Sell it Online: How to Make Money Selling on eBay, Amazon, Fiverr, & Etsy

Audio Books by Nick Vulich

eBay 2014: Why Your Stuff Isn't Selling And What You Can Do About It

Freaking Idiots guide to Selling on eBay: How anyone can make $100 or more everyday selling on eBay

Made in the USA
Monee, IL
18 July 2021

73822146R00042